Reading Primers
R_0 & R_1

Caleb Gattegno

Educational Solutions Worldwide Inc.

Published separately in 1977. Compiled and reprinted in 2009.

Copyright © 1977-2009 Educational Solutions Worldwide Inc.
First Edition
Author: Caleb Gattegno
All rights reserved
ISBN 978-0-87825-036-3

Educational Solutions Worldwide Inc.
2nd Floor 99 University Place, New York, N.Y. 10003-4555
www.EducationalSolutions.com

Table of Contents

Reading Primer R0

Word Building Table 0

a

Table 0.1

4

a a a

a a a a a a

a a a a a a a

a a a a a a

a a a a a a

— a aa a   — a a aa aa

— aa aaa   — aa aa a

— a aa a a a   — aaa aa

— a a aa   — aa aa a a

— aaaa a   — aa a a

— aaa aa a   — a aaaa

— aaa aaa a   — a a aa aaa

— aa aaaa   — a aa aaa

— aa a aaaa   — aaa aaa

a   u

Table 0.2

U U U

U U U U U U

ᴜ ᴜ ᴜ ᴜ ᴜ ᴜ ᴜ

aᴜ ᴜa aaᴜ aᴜa ᴜaa

aᴜaᴜ ᴜaᴜa aaᴜᴜ ᴜᴜaa ᴜaaᴜ

ᴜᴜaaa ᴜaᴜaa aᴜaᴜa aᴜᴜaa aaaᴜᴜ

— U U UU   — UU U U

— UU U UUU   — UUU UU U

— U UU UUU   — U UUU UU

— au ua u   — U ua UU

— uau aa u   — U a aa UU

— UU U a UUU   — aau uaa aua

— auu uaa a   — uau auu u a

— aauu uaua au   — a U UU UUU

— a aa aaa a   — U U UUUU UUU

a u i

Table 0.3

12

i i i

i i i i i i

i ii iii ui iu uiu iuu uii

ai ia iia iai aii aui uia

iau iua aiu uai uiia uiai

iaai iuui iaui aiiu uiiu uiia

— i iii   — i i ii

— i ii iii   — i iii iii

— iii ii i   — ii i iii

— iii iii iiii iiiii   — a a i i

— i au uai   — auu aui ia

— u iaai   — iaai ui iu

— uiui aiai   — i u i ai

— iiaaa iuiii   — aiaiui uiaaii

— ii uu aa   — a iaaai iuui

— iiiaaa aiaiuui

14

auie

Table 0.4

16

e e e

e e e e e e

ee eee e eeeee eee ee

ei ie ea ae ue eu eei eie

eai iie iei eeai ieae uei iue eaae

eea eeae eaee aeee auei aiue aaeeuuii

— ee ee   — ee eee e

— e ee eee   — ee eee

— eee e ee   — e ee ee e

— e e ee eee   — eeeeee

— e ii ae   — ei ie aie

— aei eia aee   — aeieia ee

— ie ie ei ei

— eii iee eie

— ae ea eea aee

— euiea

— aiei iaee eai

— uei i eea

— e i a uu eiua eeuea

— aaee uuee iiee

— eeaa eeii eeuu

— eauie aeueie

a u i e o

Table 0.5

O   O   O

O   O   O   O   O   O

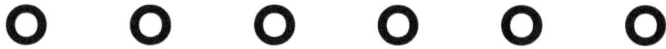

oo   o   ooo   o   oooo   o   ooooo   o

oi io ao oa uo ou oe eo eoo ooe aoo

oeo eeo eoe aeeo eoee eeoe uoeoo

eiuao eiuoa eoiuoo aeoiuo oeiuoa

21

— o o oo

— oo oo oo o

— oo o oo o oo

— oo o ooo

— ooo oo o

— o oo ooo oooo

— oi a eo oo i

— eoa uee iie

— eee ooa oei

— oaa oee oii eou

22

— ioi eoe oeo

— oi ooi oooi ooooi

— auieo uieo ieo eo o

— o oe oei oeiu oeiua

— aooaa

— aaooi uuooi eeooei

— aooae oaoai oaaou

— eieoeuea

Reading Primer R₁

Word Building Table 1

o	
e	
	s ss s
i	s
u	t tt
a	p pp

27

a u i e o

p

Table 1.1

ap　pa　up　pu　ip　pi

ep　pe　op　po

pap　pup　pip　pep　pop

— pop up　　　　　— pep up

— up up up　　　　— up pop up

— pep up pop

a   u   i   e   o

t

Table 1.2

at ta ut tu it ti

et te ot to

tat tut tit tet tot

— at it   — tot it up

— tit tat   — tat it

— tut tut tut

a u i e o

p   t

pp   tt

Table 1.3

pat	tap	pet	tep
tip	pit	putt	pitt
pot	top	pott	topp

— pat pott

— pitt pott

— pat topp

— pitt topp

— tap it   — putt it

— top it   — pop it

— tip it   — pet pup

— tap it   pop

— pop   tap it

— tip it up   pat

— pat   tip it up

— pitt   tip it up

— tip it up   pitt

a u i e o

s

Table 1.4

as sa us su is si

es se os so

— as is

a u i e o

p t s

pp tt

Table 1.5

— is it   — it is

— is it up   — it is up

— is pop up   — pop is up

— is it pat   — it is pat

— as pat is   — is it pitt

— as is pat   — it is pitt

— as it is   — is it as it is

— is pat apt

— pat is as apt as pitt is

— is pitt as apt as pat

— pat is up as is pitt

a   u   i   e   o

p   t   s   s

pp   tt   ss

's

Table 1.6

as   us   is   es   os

ass   uss   iss   ess   oss

sis   ses   sess   sus   suss

tess   pass   sit   sat   set   sip   sap

sits   sets   sips   saps

– pat's   – pitt's   – it's

– it's pat   – it's pitt   – it's pop

— pass it   — pat's pet

— pitt's pot   — it's pat's pop

— pass us   — pass us up

— as it is us   — pat is up

— pat's pet is up

— is pat's pet up

— is it pat's pot — it is

— it is pat pott   — is it

— sit up pat   — pat sits up

— pat sat up

— set it up   pat — pat sets it up

— set it up   tess

— pat   it is sap

— pitt saps it   — tess sips pop

42

pets pots pits pats putts tops

tips taps stop spot spit spat

spits step upset spots stops steps

spats test past pest

— pat is upset

— it is past

— stop it pat

— pat sips pop

— pat spat

— tess steps up

— pat upsets pop

— pat upsets pop's pot

— pat is as upset at tess

— is pat as upset at pitt

— is pat upset

— stop pat stop

— pat spots us

— pitt tests us

— pat spits at spots

— step it up, pat

— tess tests pat

Word Building Table 2

a u i e o a l

e

's   m

'm

Table 2.1

am	mat	top	mist	miss
sam	met	mast	mitt	pump
pam	tim	must	mess	sum

misses	messes	passes
stamp	mumps	stump
mom's	tom's	pam's

— it is mom's   — I'm a mess

— I miss pop   — mess it up

— pat's stamps   — sum it up

— sam's mitt

— I pat pat

— tim must sit

— sam sat at a pump

— miss pam stops it

— a map is a must

— pitt is up a mast

— pat is at mass

— tom met tim at pam's

— pop misses passes

— as pam passes it, pat sips it up

— tom passes a stump

— tom's puppet sits up

— it is mumps

— pop mops messes

— I mess it up

a u i e o a y l
o e

m m   n   y

          n n

Table 2.2

an	on	in	tan	not	ant
pan	ten	pin	sun	son	ton
net	tin	men	man	nap	pen
yet	yes	tent	sent	nut	yam

mommy   puppy   sunny   penny   yummy

assist   assistant

— sam is a man

— mom sent pam in

— I'm not in it

— I spent it

— pat is not a man

— pam is in a mess

— it is ten past ten

— tim is not ten yet

— sum it up, mom

— an ant is in sam's pants

— sam sat on a mat in the sun

— as I sat up, a man set it up

— must tom sit on a top

— it's a pin in sam's pants

— sam is a pest, tom a nut

— I'm not a nut, I'm a man

— pat assists tom on a test

— I am pat's assistant

— ten men sat on ten stumps in a tent

— pop sent pam stamps in a set

— stamps tempt pam

— as sam met pat at tom's, tim met pam

— tommy is tom's son

— a yam is yummy

— mom sent pants, pop stamps, tim pens, sam pins, pat nuts

— nasty tommy steps on maps

— at ten, tim is not a man

— is it a net   — it is a net
  it's an ant net

— sam misses ten attempts

— is a sun a son   — it is not
  a sun is a sun, a son a son

— is a sum a sun, a sun a sum

— timmy, tommy, sammy, penny, patty, mommy
  sat on a mat in pam's tent

— tom spent a penny at sam's

— assistants, assist pop stamp

— pam's puppy naps on a step

www.ingramcontent.com/pod-product-compliance
Lightning Source LLC
Chambersburg PA
CBHW080938040426
42443CB00015B/3458